I0484976

Customer Relationship Management

:: Author ::

Dr. Chirag V. Raval

(M.COM., M.phil, Ph.D)

**Assistant Professor,
AIMS College of Management & Technology,
AIMS Education Campus,Vadtal Vidyanagar Road,
Bakrol- 388 315, Dist. Anand, Gujarat.**

PUBLISHED BY

**Chakravarti Siddharaj Jaysinh International
Publishing House**
H.Q. At & Po. Chaveli., Ta- Chansma,
Dist- Patan, North Gujarat, India, Asia.
www.iphouseindia.com

First Publication: 15th December, 2014

Copyright: Author

(c) **Dr. Chirag V. Raval**

ISBN:- 978-15-08473-04-6

Price: Rs.750/- INDIA

$ 15 OUTSIDE INDIA

PUBLISHED BY

Chakravarti Siddharaj Jaysinh International Publishing House
HQ. At & Po. Chaveli., Ta- Chansma,
Dist- Patan, North Gujarat, India, Asia.
www.iphouseindia.com

Content

Sr.no	Particulars	Page no.
Unit 01	Conceptual Foundation	1
Unit 02	Implementation, Tools of Customer Relationship Management	31
Unit 03	E-CRM	40
Unit 04	Customer Relationship Management Practices	57

Unit: 1

Conceptual Foundation

Concept, Definition, Benefits, Customer Life Cycle Value, Winning Markets through effective customer relationship management, Globalization of Customer Relationship Management.

Introduction:

CRM is best tool of to build a powerful customer experience as the most competitive weapon around our businesses. CRM invert the pyramid for achieving success in businesses in the 21st century. Through CRM companies now have a better framework for choosing strategies and actions based on which would provide the best return on Marketing investments.

CRM stands for **Customer Relationship Management**. It is a process or methodology used to learn more about customers' needs and behaviors in order to develop stronger relationships with them. There are many technological components to CRM, but thinking about CRM Software in primarily technological terms is a mistake. The more useful way to think about CRM is as a process that will help bring together lots of pieces of information about customers, sales, marketing effectiveness, responsiveness and market trends.

CRM helps businesses use technology and human resources to gain insight into the behavior of customers and the value of those customers.

Customer Relationship Management

Customer Relationship Management (CRM) employs people, technology, tools, processes and activities to increase customer retention and a firm's profitability. Early CRM use was fraught with problems, as many firms applied CRM inappropriately. In recent years, however, firms have become selective and prudent with their CRM investments, and many of them are now reporting success with CRM.

Customer relationship management (CRM) is a combination of organizational strategy, information systems, and technology that is focused on providing better customer service. CRM uses emerging technology that allows organizations to provide fast and effective customer service by developing a relationship with each customer through the effective use of customer database information systems. The objectives of CRM are to acquire new customers, retain the right current customers, and grow the relationship with an organization's existing customers. An integrated business model that ties together technology, information systems, and business processes along the entire value chain of an organization is critical to the success of CRM.

CRM can also be considered a corporate strategy because it is a fundamental approach to doing business. The goal is to be customer-focused and customer-driven, running all aspects of the business to satisfy the customers by addressing their requirements for products and by providing high-quality, responsive customer service. Companies that adopt this approach are called customer-centric, rather than product-centric.

To be customer-centric, companies need to collect and store meaningful information in a comprehensive customer database. A customer database is an organized collection of information about individual customers or prospects. The database must be current, accessible, and actionable in order to support the generation of leads for new customers while supporting sales and the maintenance of current customer relationships. Smart organizations are collecting information every time a customer comes into contact with the organization. Based on what they know about the individual customer, organizations can customize market offerings, services, programs, messages, and choice of media.

A customer database ideally would contain the customer's history of past purchases, demographics, activities/interests/ opinions, preferred media, and other useful information. Also, this database should be available to any organizational units that have contact with the customer.

CRM has also grown in scope. CRM initially referred to technological initiatives to make call centers less expensive and more efficient. Now, a lot of organizations are looking at more macro organizational changes. Organizations are now asking how they can change their business processes to use the customer data that they have gathered. CRM is changing into a business process instead of just a technology process.

Defining CRM

Customer Relationship Marketing is a practice that encompasses all marketing activities directed toward establishing, developing, and maintaining successful customer relationships. The focus of relationship marketing is on developing long-term relationships and improving corporate performance through customer loyalty and customer retention.

Customer Relationship Management (CRM) as the name suggests, the primary focal point is placed on the customer. The key objective is to increase customer value over time by increasing customer loyalty. If a company develops better customer relationships, it also improves business processes as well as its profits. In general, CRM is a more efficient automated method used to connect and improve all areas of business to focus on creating strong customer relationships. All forces are coupled together to save, improve, and acquire greater business to customer relationships. The most common areas of business that are positively affected include marketing, sales, and customer service strategies.

CRM helps create time efficiency and savings on both sides of the business spectrum. Through correct implementation and use of CRM solutions, companies gain a better understanding of their strongest and weakest areas and how they can improve upon these. Therefore, customers gain better products and services from their businesses of choice. In order to achieve better insight on CRM, it is essential to consider all of its components.

CRM- meaning

Customer relationship management (CRM) is a business strategy that spans your entire organization from front office to back-office. It is a commitment you make to put customers at the heart of your enterprise. The right CRM strategy and solutions can help you securely, reliably and consistently:

- Delight your customers every time they interact with your business by empowering them with anytime, anywhere, and any channel access to accurate information and more personalized service.

- Reach more customers more effectively, increase customer retention and boost customer loyalty by leveraging opportunities to up-sell and cross-sell and driving repeat business at lower cost.

- Drive improvements in business performance by providing your customers with the ability to access more information through self-service and assisted-service capabilities when it is convenient for them.

- Enable virtualization in your enterprise as more of your people and resources extend beyond your offices and around the world.

- Balance sophisticated functionality with rapid implementation and effective support for a faster return on your CRM investment.

Today's customers face a growing range of choices in the products and services they can buy. They base their choices on their perception of quality, value, and service. Each consumer has a specific behavior. But buying habits are sometimes difficult to understand. Therefore companies always want to gain some insight about consumer behavior and habits in order to better control this behavior. Having an impact on consumer behavior means being able to change consumer's perception of the product or service, to establish a relation between the company and its clients.

What is Customer Relationship Management (CRM)?

CRM entails all aspects of interaction a company has with its customer, whether it is sales or service related. It even uses technology to streamline processes that impact customer loyalty, service delivery and quality management.

Today, businesses are facing an aggressive competition and they have to make Efforts to survive in a competitive and uncertain market place. People have realized that managing Customer relationships is a very important factor for their success. Customer relationship management (CRM) is a strategy that can help them to build long-lasting relationships with their customers and increase their profits through the right management system and the application of customer-focused strategies.

"Customer is the most important person for a business. He is not an interruption to our work but the purpose of it. He is not an outsider; he is a part of it. We are not doing him a favour; he is doing us a favour by giving us an opportunity to serve him."(By Mahatma Gandhi)

It has grown mainstream and is being implemented in a wide range of companies and organizations such as manufacturing, financial services, transportation and distribution, medical services and products, consumer package goods and others. This explosive growth of CRM reflects the intersection of genuine market need and enabling technology. And, in this growth period, the impetus for CRM is shifting from an emphasis on efficiency, i.e., doing more things faster with less cost, to effectiveness, i.e., doing things better for increased revenue with a high "return on relationships (ROR)".

According to Chaudhuri and Shainesh (2001)-A CRM programmer requires a clear understanding and commitment to the company's customers, vigilant adherence to detailed goals, commitment from both executives and line workers, and a constant awareness of the customer's view point. Customer relationship management is about more than simply managing customers and monitoring their behavior or attitude. CRM has the potential to change a customer's relations with a company and increase revenues in the bargain. Furthermore it helps to know the customers well-enough to decide whom to choose and whom to lose.

The objective of CRM (customer relationship management) is to recognize and treat each and every customer as an individual. It is very essential for any business to know that how to differentiate customer treatment according to an individual preferences. For differentiate customer treatment, the companies use personalized service and customized products which make some customers feel special and others simply appreciate good behavior. It humanizes their purchase or service request or complaint. Personalization and customization doesn't mean maintaining only customer loyalty, but also driving purchases higher.

Getting closer to customers and effectively responding to their needs is a great way to boost their loyalty and encourage deeper business relationship. The task of getting and retaining customers requires even greater skill and effort. The business needs to ensure that the service works as the customer actually wants it to, and the customers want to do business in 'their' way, not to be forced to do it in the enterprise's way. Most companies consider them customer-focused and believe that in being so they are servicing the customer. But eventually, being customer focused means to have a consistent, dependable and convenient interaction with customers in every encounter. CRM technologies focus on managing all interactions that an organization has with its customers, in order to leverage the data in a variety of business applications.

Where a profitable relationship already exists, CRM can especially boost superior service at a lower cost. In addition to this it helps to serve customer's unspoken needs.

Generally speaking, the five needs of customers are:-

(a) Service

(b) Price

(c) Quality

(d) Action and

(e) Appreciation.   (By Raghunath & Shields 2001)

Apart from these, there would be needs, which even the customers have not taken care of, but which, if would have satisfied will lead to higher customer loyalty. CRM, if practiced properly might lead to cross-selling and up selling of products and services. Cross-selling means selling the right product to the right customer. One other relevant and important attribute of CRM is its ability to help in the ego-mending of customers. This, if practiced efficiently, soothes the customer's negative emotions he could have, due to the non-attainment of his expectations regarding the product or the service.

Benefits of CRM

Using CRM, a business can:-

> Provide better customer service

> Increase customer revenues

> Discover new customers

> Cross sell/Up Sell products more effectively

> Help sales staff close deals faster

> Make call centers more efficient

➢ Simplify marketing and sales processes

Generally, following are the type of data a CRM project includes (Lemon, et al, 2002):

➢ Responses to campaigns

➢ Shipping and fulfillment dates

➢ Sales and purchase data

➢ Account information

➢ Web registration data

➢ Service and support records

➢ Demographic data

➢ Web sales data

Customer Life Cycle Value

Customer value management is managing each customer relationship with the goal of achieving maximum lifetime profit from the entire customer base. Customer value management enables companies to take full advantage of the economics of loyalty by increasing retention, reducing risk, and amortizing acquisition costs over a longer and more profitable period of engagement. Although customer value management seeks to increase the aggregate value of the customer base, this is accomplished customer by customer. Not every individual customer will be profitable, but each must be managed to maximize overall profit, even when the management consists of identifying which customers have little value to the business, and focusing development and retention efforts elsewhere.

CVM shifts the focus of the enterprise from managing products or marketing campaigns to managing the profitability of each individual customer over the entire life of the relationship. While CVM can and does lead to better product offerings and more targeted campaigns, a customer value manager will ask different questions than a traditional marketing manager. Instead of asking, "Who will respond to a 10% off promotion?", a customer value manager is driven to understand, "Who is this customer, and what can I offer to increase their lifetime value?".

Making this shift requires companies to move from giving lip service to one-to-one marketing to actually developing the analytical and operational capabilities to do it. But those that do so can expect increased profits, not only in the short term, but for years to come.

Three "Rs" of the CVM Cycle

The customer value management cycle can be broken down into three stages:

• Right customers (acquisition)

• Right relationship (development)

• Right retention (keeping valuable customers)

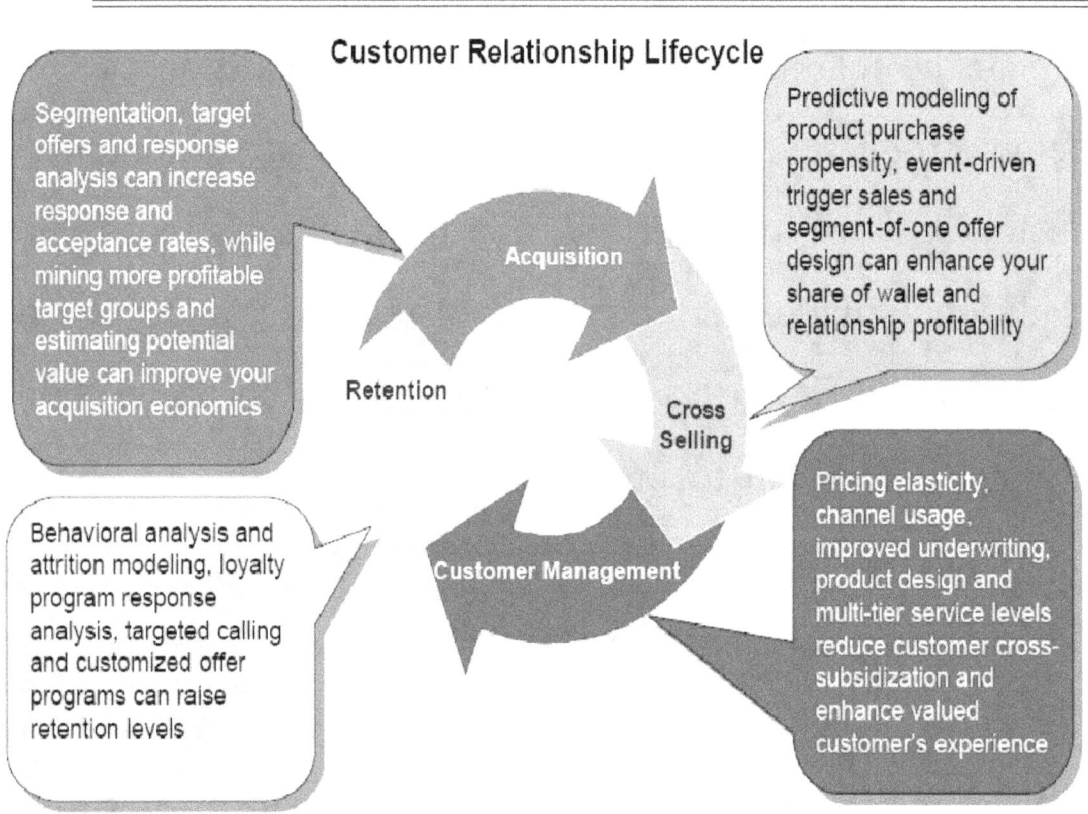

Right Customers

The customer value management cycle starts with acquiring the customers who will be most valuable to your business. Who are these customers? Most often those who will do repeat business with your company for a long time. In The Loyalty Effect, Reichheld cites examples of how long a customer must stay in order to pay for the cost of acquisition. In many industries the break-even period is a year or more, and rising. Companies can no longer afford to indiscriminately recruit customers without examining their long-term value. All customers are not equal. Even a customer that is high-value to a competitor might well be unprofitable for you. For example, there are profitable insurance companies that specialize in safe drivers, as well as those who focus on drivers with higher risk. A "good driver" company would be acquiring the wrong customers by placing ads in racing car magazines. Because customer acquisition is so costly, effective customer value management requires your company to develop the analytical capabilities to identify customers who will be loyal and profitable, not just for your industry, but for your specific company. Your best source of intelligence about the customers you want is deep analysis of your current customers – the people on whom you already have extensive data. Fine-grained segmentation and analysis of your customer base reveals hidden characteristics and trends that affect value. Perhaps certain customers have been regarded as low-value because they make only small purchases. Finer segmentation that includes frequency of purchase might reveal that a subset of these customers have a very high lifetime value, because they have regularly made these small purchases every week for the past ten years. Such deep understanding of who are your best customers, and why, enables you to go after the new customers your company can most profitably serve.

Right Customers

Right Relationship

Right Retention

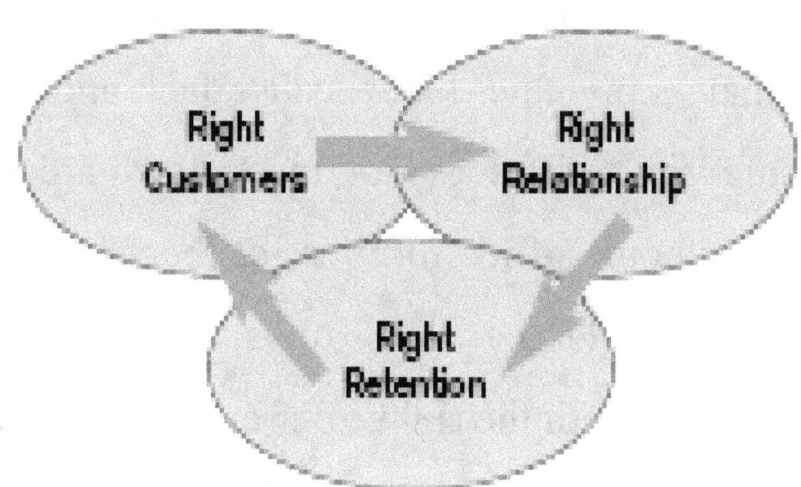

customer value.

Business Objects • Customer Value Management

Customer vintage analysis – examining the loyalty and profitability of customers who joined at different times through different channels – adds insight into where your best customers come from. Perhaps customers who joined during a price promotion left quickly, while those who joined after attending an educational seminar stayed. This time-based analysis is key to knowing which acquisition strategies are worth repeating, and which are long-term money losers hiding behind a mask of high recruitment rates.

Right Relationship

Even with the most well chosen customers, managers must develop the relationship. Customers who do don't receive the right touch or get too many conflicting offers lose rather than gain value. Just because Jack and Frank live in the same zip code does not mean they are both in the market for home office furniture at the same time. Ideally marketers would be able to spot these differences, targeting Jack with the right offer at the right time, without annoying Frank with another promotion for something he does not want.

For any business, the right relationship is one that maximizes that customer's lifetime value.

A simplified view of customer lifetime value is:

LTV = purchase size x frequency x duration So the businesses goal of customer relationship management is to increase the size and frequency of purchases and extend how long the customer continues to buy. Since marketers can't know the duration of a relationship until it is over, they use loyalty measures to estimate how long customers will stay.

Customers do repeat business with vendors that understand and respond to their individual needs, and respond when those needs change. To improve customer value, marketers must understand differences between their customers, and track how each individual evolves over time. The specific actions managers should take depend on the value of the customer.

For high-value customers, managers should work to cement loyalty, extending the length of an already profitable relationship. The LTV of a customer that makes large purchases regularly for ten years is significantly more than that of a customer who makes the same purchases for only Five years.

Customers that are not currently high-value may still have high potential for growth in any of the three parts of the value equation. Telling these customers apart from those who will never grow in value represents a significant analytical challenge. Unless marketers can distinguish high potential customers from ones who will always be low-value, companies will waste resources trying to develop customers who will never grow.

One often-ignored group of high potential is former high-value customers who have migrated downward. These customers are often still high value, bust most of that value has simply been transferred to a competitor. Most companies cannot easily identify these individuals because they value customers based on a point in time, with no reference to previous value and history. If Jill and Jim each were gold segment customers until last month, but have transferred some of their business to a competitor, the company may well not notice if enough customers have entered the gold segment to replace them and kept the total number of gold customers steady. The company needs deeper analysis to spot Jill and Jim's downward migration and to work on restoring their value. Companies that develop the capability to track changes in the value of individual customers can guard against competitive attacks and respond quickly to changing customer behavior to maintain and grow customer value.

Right Retention

Effective retention means retaining the right customers, not every customer. Managers need to focus their retention actions on customers with the highest lifetime value. Spending precious resources to retain marginally profitable or unprofitable customers actually hurts the overall value of the customer base, especially if these retention efforts succeed. Right retention is therefore rooted in knowing which individuals are most valuable, and why. Accurately analyzing lifetime value helps managers take the long view, giving equal weight to customers who are already doing a high volume of business and those who purchases are modest, but whose actions indicate loyalty and profitability over time. Having identified the customers worth keeping, managers must ensure that their retention strategies maintain value, not erode it.

According to Reichheld, one reason loyal customers are more profitable is that they are less price-sensitive. Therefore managers should retain these loyal customers through incentives other than price, such as special recognition and premium levels of service. Even if heavy discounting does retain high-value customers, they train customers to become more price sensitive and therefore less valuable.

Customer value management offers a roadmap to acquiring, developing and retaining your most valuable customers. Taking the journey shown on the map is not free. Managers who wish to\ reap increased customer value must pay more than lip service to the idea of being customer driven. They must develop the analytical capability to understand their customers as individuals, and integrate this customer intelligence into their operational systems to enable immediate response to each customer's changing behavior and value. The reward for making this investment is sustained and increasingly profitable relationships, potentially the most enduring asset in today's ever-changing business climate. By deepening and lengthening customer relationships, your business can drive increased revenue from its customer base, even as products and sales channels continue to evolve.

Winning Markets through effective customer relationship management

1. Call centers: These are organizations which deal directly to the customer interactions. These are otherwise known as "Customer Care Centre" or "Contact Centre" indicating more technological sophistication and multichannel support. Call centre technologies   entered

the market place to effectively alleviate some of the repeat work and increase efficiencies, allowing companies to handle escalating call volumes. Customer Service Representatives (CSRs) could look up similar calls and resolutions while a customer was on the phone, without having to repeat research. The software tools being used in the call-centers also provide forecasting of call volumes to ensure adequate call centre staffing. (Lemon, et al, 2002)

2. Web based self-service: The customers themselves, without the help of a live person can resolve their problems or find out answers to their queries using the web. This model is founded on the principle of enabling customers, partners and employees to obtain information's or conduct transactions directly over the internet, avoiding time-consuming and costly traditional processes involving multiple verbal or written interactions. It provides control, performance, convenience and efficiency. (Chaudhuri & Shainesh 2001)

3. Customer satisfaction measurement: Survey mails are the major way for companies to monitor customer

satisfaction. Nowadays, these survey forms are even personalized to specific customers or customer groups. Responses are input into customer databases and included as part of individual customer profiles. Such tracking of customer satisfaction over time enables a company to fine tune how it communicates with its customers according to their preferences. (Mohan Babu, 2003) Now, the paper based surveys are giving way to electronic surveys.

4. Call-scripting: Automatic scripts generated for customer service representatives, based on an individual customer's segment and/or customer profile contents. Scripts remove the guess work from determining how to respond to a customer query or complaint, guiding representatives through a dialogue with the customer and thus optimizing discrete customer interactions.

5. Cyber agents: This is a kind of an improved or modified form of the concept of self-service. Cyber agents are 'lifelike representatives' normally depicted on a company's web site as a real person. This attempt to pull together the best of both personalization and advanced technology. It is given a personality and is having facial expressions and

volume. Usually a cyber agent addresses the web visitor with his/her first name. It can draw from the wealth of detailed information to answer basic FAQs as well as guide a customer to the appropriate screen for a definite purpose/action. (Raghunath & Shields 2001)

6. Web site: It is the efficient and effective use of worldwide web for providing information to the customers, by a company who had created that site, in a hassle-free manner. The main advantage of a web site is its 24 hours accessibility.

Usually gathering information from the site is a simple task and is cost-effective. In the US and in the developed countries web is extensively used. In the case of monetary transactions, if it is a high involvement activity most of the customers prefer the offline mode mainly due to their concern over security problems in monetary transactions, through the net.

a) CRM's ability to impact corporate strategy:

Without a corporate strategy, giving emphasis to a customer-centric approach, no CRM initiative can be made fully successful.

b) Successful technology integration:

The technology which has been used across different departments of an enterprise should be integrated to give a comprehensive and successful CRM application.

c) Enhanced strategic partnerships:

For a good CRM implementation, there should be a co-ordinate effort among the different partners to the enterprise.

d) Assimilation of CRM related technologies:

Those who are responsible for the CRM activities should thoroughly be conversant with the technological aspects of that particular technique. Otherwise, misuse or under utilization of these technologies may take place resulting in partial or full failure of those activities.

Globalization of Customer Relationship Management

The globalization of markets has been one of the major business developments in the last three decades. Craig and Douglas contend that choosing not to participate in global markets is no longer optional. The pressure of global competition impacts every domestic market as well as international markets. Marketplaces are transitioning to demand side approaches with a focus on customer needs and wants. Customer Relationship Management (CRM) thus should assume a central sole in the marketing management of global products and services. The impact of globalization on CRM however represents an under researched area.

The impact of global marketing is particularly noticeable in New Zealand. In less than ten years commencing in the mid 1980s. New Zealand moved from being a highly regulated economy to one of the worlds least regulated. Lessons taken from the New Zealand market can potentially be compared with, or even implemented in, much larger markets, particularly in countries experiencing deregulation; it may also be of benefit to smaller countries espousing similar intent, and may useful serve as a set of guidelines for both types of economies.

It is clear tht global marketing presents substantial challenges. Among these are that market segmentation and positioning strategies may need diverge widely to accommodate customer needs and preferences. The structures of competitive environments may also vary widely from country to country, as may product life cycle stage. These factors will inevitably rebound on CRM strategies. It also begs the questions of whether these strategies can be 'globalized' and whether globalized CRM strategies are more or less effective than strategy tailors specifically for local markets.

Marketing itself is now concerned with understanding of target customers and develops the value propositions that customers want and need, and then creating the marketing approach. This does not mean that this approach is followed by international firms, certain other factors, for example corporate edict, may control how country strategic business units approach marketing and marketing communication.

CONCLUSION

We conclude by saying that CRM is best tool of to build a powerful customer experience as the most competitive weapon around our businesses. CRM invert the pyramid for achieving success in businesses in the 21st

century and CRM as the prime focal weapon to win over your customer and competition.

IF YOU WANT TO DRIVE THE COMPETITION CRAZY, IGNORE YOUR COMPETITORS AND CONCENTRATE ON YOUR CUSTOMER'S ONE ON ONE.

Unit: 2

Implementation, Tools of Customer Relationship Management

Approaches to successful Customer Relationship Management, Integration of customer Relationship Management, Ways to manage customer relationship

Approaches to successful Customer Relationship Management

Endeavoring to make sure that appropriate vendor selection takes place should also be one of Management's efforts. Placing the right person in control of the entire CRM process or placing a separate department to deal with the CRM efforts right upto the results is mandatory and of supreme importance to managerial functions.

> ➢ Customer contact is also essential for top management. Knowing the ins and outs of the customer process as well as maintaining personal contact is essential. In some areas this may not be possible to achieve. In this instant Management can opt to study the customer data made available to them

through the CRM software and use it to identify customer preferences and act accordingly.

➢ For CRM, Management should also provide sufficient motivation to employees before focusing on a customer oriented strategy. Sufficient time gap should be allotted for the required ROI as well as the expected affect on customer retention.

➢ Ensuring that the employees dealing with the CRM process have sufficient knowledge about it and identifying areas of training and making sure that these areas are covered with adequate training methods is the work of Management. CRM managing software can also be beneficial to Management seeking to help employees engaged in the CRM process.

➢ It is essential that managers find out what the main issues of concern are where customers are concerned, pay adequate attention to the collation of customer data and study that data in an effort to find out more about the customer.

> CRM managing software gives adequate support to people involved in the CRM process. Establishing the right authority and responsibility to carry out the CRM process, ensuring that they have adequate resources at their disposal and making sure a separate CRM budget is implemented is mandatory. It is imperative that top Management get directly involved in the CRM process.

> Periodical monitoring of achievements, failures, cost adherence etc is essential as managerial functions to ensure CRM success. It is vital to management functions as it ensures that the CRM process is going as planned. Any deviation should be immediately identified and corrected.

> An established CRM grievance cell should be administered with the option of bringing in outside resources if required and CRM fails. This should be made ample use of for the identification of any CRM problems and the offering of solutions for CRM problems.

It is the responsibility of management to identify organization objectives, communicate these objectives to the necessary employees, employ CRM managing software and basically serve to ensure that employees dealing with the CRM implementation are adequately educated.

Integration of customer Relationship Management

The process of extracting customer data from legacy systems (i.e., the property management system) and integrating the entire database in the property that contains guest information is complex and time-consuming. The data sources may include guest history, external guest profiling systems, restaurant club programs, sales and catering system information and other data.

1. Customer profiling:

Demographic and Psychographic information can be appended to a large percentage of the customer database. This is followed by the implementation of effective marketing programs to attract similar customers to build revenue.

2. Direct marketing:

The utilization of the integrated customer information for direct marketing offers is the goldmine of any CRM effort. Highly profitable offers can provide business during slow periods. These offers can be communicated via mail or e-mail.

3. Best customer/extraordinary service:

The Mecca of all is to understand if the most profitable customers are the most satisfied. This involves very detailed satisfaction analysis, combined with valid financial data about each customer – all appended to the customer database. It's uncertain whether anyone is there in the hospitality industry, but certainly companies are getting very close to understanding the most profitable customers and most profitable micro-markets. The immediate tactical example of this is can be found in well utilized sales and catering systems, which integrate the profitability of groups and meetings. Linking the meeting planner satisfaction to each of these sales and catering accounts is the first step in making sure that your best customers are most satisfied.

CRM is not a buzzword program, like so many that have gone before. It is the integration of all the elements that hospitality has focused on forever:

1. Personally recognizing customers;

2. Offering appropriate value and great service to encourage repeat business;

3. Insuring that employee and guest satisfaction continues to improve; and

4. Beating the competition by offering a better product, competing on the service experience rather than price alone.

Like a dog chasing a truck, once you've caught it – what are you going to do with it? This is the analogy posed by Peter Aeby, general manager of the legendary Brown Palace Hotel in Denver and the chairman of Preferred Hotels & Resorts Worldwide. Aeby is referring to the mass of information that major hospitality organizations are now able to collect about customers. How is it possible to make all this information actionable? And, with an understanding of labor shortages, high turnover and lack of computer integration, how does a hotel manager tactically utilize available tools to improve the frontline experience? How does that same manager build revenues and customer loyalty from this data?

Ways to manage customer relationship

In today's competitive world , achieving total customer satisfaction/ delighting customer is a key element in setting the business goals and objectives of the corporate. Improving performance in service delivery and responsiveness to the customers has become a source of competitive advantage in many industry and service sectors. Customer Relationship Management is being increasingly used to identify, attract, and retain most valuable customers that help businesses to sustain profitable growth. Successful companies are achieving long term performance in customer relationship management by gaining deep insights about their customers which helps them design product/ service offerings that match or exceed the customer expectations which in turn help in building customer trust and gain loyalty. Following are Ways to manage customer relationship

e) CRM's ability to impact corporate strategy:

Without a corporate strategy, giving emphasis to a customer-centric approach, no CRM initiative can be made fully successful.

f) Successful technology integration:

The technology which has been used across different departments of an enterprise should be integrated to give a comprehensive and successful CRM application.

g) Enhanced strategic partnerships:

For a good CRM implementation, there should be a co-ordinate effort among the different partners to the enterprise.

h) Assimilation of CRM related technologies:

Those who are responsible for the CRM activities should thoroughly be conversant with the technological aspects of that particular technique. Otherwise, misuse or under utilization of these technologies may take place resulting in partial or full failure of those activities.

CRM projects require careful planning and implementation. To be successful, CRM involves major cultural and organizational changes that will meet with a lot of resistance. CRM should be enterprise-wide in scale and scope. However, it is usually better to take an incremental approach starting with a CRM pilot. Once the pilot succeeds, then introducing one CRM application at a time is recommended. Also, it is important to be skeptical of vendor claims and to know that user expectations for CRM are often unreasonable.

Unit: 3

E-CRM: Meaning, Concept, Evolution of E-CRM, Business intelligence System, Changing patterns of ECRM solutions in the future

E-CRM

E-CRM is the term that some people have used to describe the customer facing portion of the CRM. The term usually implies capabilities like self service knowledge bases, automated email response, personalization of web content, online product, bundling and pricing etc. E-CRM gives the internet users the ability to interact with the business through their preferred communication channel and it allows the business to offset expensive customer service agents with technology. So the value is largely one of improved customer satisfaction and reduced cost through improved customers satisfaction and reduced cost through imp[roved efficiency.

About Customer Relationship Management - CRM

The generally accepted purpose of Customer Relationship Management (CRM) is to enable organizations to better serve its customers through the introduction of reliable processes and procedures for interacting with those customers.

In today's competitive business environment, a successful CRM strategy cannot be implemented by only installing and integrating a software package designed to support CRM processes. A holistic approach to CRM is vital for an effective and efficient CRM policy. This approach includes training of employees, a modification of business processes based on customers' needs and an adoption of relevant IT-systems (including soft- and maybe hardware) and/or usage of IT-Services that enable the organization or company to follow its CRM strategy. CRM-Services can even redundant the acquisition of additional hardware or CRM software-licenses.

The term CRM is used to describe either the software or the whole business strategy oriented on customer needs. The second one is the description which is correct. The main misconception of CRM is that it is only software, instead of whole business strategy.

Major areas of CRM focus on service automated processes, personal information gathering and processing, and self-service. It attempts to integrate and automate the various customer serving processes within a company.

There are three parts of application architecture of CRM:

1. Operational - automation to the basic business processes (marketing, sales, service)

2. Analytical - support to analyse customer behaviour, implements business intelligence alike technology

3. Cooperational - ensures the contact with customers (phone, email, fax, web...)

Operational part of CRM typically involves three general areas of business. They are (according to Gartner Group) an Enterprise marketing automation (EMA), Sales force automation (SFA) and a Customer service and support (CSS). The marketing information part provides information about the business environment, including competitors, industry trends, and macro environmental variables. The sales force management part automates some of the company's sales and sales force management functions. It keeps track of customer preferences, buying habits, and demographics, and also sales staff performance. The customer service part automates some service requests, complaints, product returns, and information requests.

Integrated CRM software is often also known as "front office solutions." This is because they deal directly with the customer.

Many call centers use CRM software to store all of their customer's details. When a customer calls, the system can be used to retrieve and store information relevant to the customer. By serving the customer quickly and efficiently, and also keeping all information on a customer in one place, a company aims to make cost savings, and also encourage new customers.

CRM solutions can also be used to allow customers to perform their own service via a variety of communication channels. For example, you might be able to check your bank balance via your WAP phone without ever having to talk to a person, saving money for the company, and saving you time.

Evolution of CRM

Customer Relationship Management (CRM) is one of those magnificent concepts that swept the business world in the 1990's with the promise of forever changing the way businesses small and large interacted with their customer bases. In the short term, however, it proved to be an unwieldy process that was better in theory than in practice for a variety of reasons. First among these was that it was simply so difficult and expensive to track and keep the high volume of records needed accurately and constantly update them.

In the last several years, however, newer software systems and advanced tracking features have vastly improved CRM capabilities and the real promise of CRM is becoming a reality. As the price of newer, more customizable Internet solutions have hit the marketplace; competition has driven the prices down so that even relatively small businesses are reaping the benefits of some custom CRM programs.

In the beginning…

The 1980's saw the emergence of database marketing, which was simply a catch phrase to define the practice of setting up customer service groups to speak individually to all of a company's customers.

In the case of larger, key clients it was a valuable tool for keeping the lines of communication open and tailoring service to the clients needs. In the case of smaller clients, however, it tended to provide repetitive, survey-like information that cluttered databases and didn't provide much insight. As companies began tracking database information, they realized that the bare bones were all that was needed in most cases: what they buy regularly, what they spend, what they do.

Advances in the 1990's

In the 1990's companies began to improve on Customer Relationship Management by making it more of a two-way street. Instead of simply gathering data for their own use, they began giving back to their customers not only in terms of the obvious goal of improved customer service, but in incentives, gifts and other perks for customer loyalty.

This was the beginning of the now familiar frequent flyer programs, bonus points on credit cards and a host of other resources that are based on CRM tracking of customer activity and spending patterns. CRM was now being used as a way to increase sales passively as well as through active improvement of customer service.

E CRM or Web based CRM

e-CRM application in hotel industry are straddling across business functions to retain, capture and capitalize on customer data, i.e. integrating all aspects of business process and systems by keeping the customers as the core. e-CRM projects are no longer viewed as stand-alone implementations but are now being increasingly pursued in context of larger business objectives and core strategic agendas. Corporations realize that the true values of their customers in down turn are the ones that will be equipped, tied over the slump and jump start, consolidate and thrive.

Although there are now many software suppliers for CRM, it began back in 1993 when Tom Siebel founded Siebel Systems Inc. Use of the term CRM is traced back to that period. In the mid-1990s CRM was originally sold as a guaranteed way to turn customer data into increased sales performance and higher profits by delivering new insights into customer behaviors and identifying hidden buying patterns buried in customer databases. Instead, CRM was one of the biggest disappointments of the 1990s. Some estimates have put CRM failure rates as high as 75 percent. But more than a decade later, more firms in the United States and Europe are appearing willing to give CRM another try. A 2005 study by the Gartner Group, found 60 percent of midsize businesses intended to adopt or expand their CRM usage over the next two years. Why the interest? Partially the renewed interest is due to a large number of CRM vendors that are offering more targeted solutions with a wider range of prices and more accountability.

Even though CRM started in the mid-1990s, it has already gone through several overlapping stages. Originally focused on automation of existing marketing processes, CRM has made a major leap forward to a customer-driven, business process management orientation.

The first stage began when firms purchased and implemented single-function client/server systems to support a particular group of employees such as the sales force, the call center representatives, or the marketing department. CRM initially meant applying automation to existing marketing activities and processes. However, automating poorly performing activities or processes did little to improve the quality of the return on investment.

In the second stage, organizations demanded more cross-functional integration to create a holistic view of their customers' relationships. Also, the integrated system's goal was to provide a single-face to the customer by enabling employees to work from a common set of customer information gathered from demographics, Web hits, product inquiries, sales calls, etc. Cross-functional integration allowed the whole organization to take responsibility for customer satisfaction and allowed for better predictive models to improve cross-selling and improved products and delivery options.

The third stage of CRM was heavily influenced by the Internet. Customer self-service and Internet-based systems became the next big thing in CRM. However, there were obstacles caused by a lack of seamless integration into the organization's operational systems and a lack of integration across customer touch points such as call centers, web transactions, and other various interactions. By rethinking the quality and effectiveness of customer-related processes, many organizations began to eliminate unnecessary activities, improve out-dated processes, and redesign systems that had failed to deliver the desired outcomes. In this stage, the big CRM vendors used new Internet-based systems to extend the reach of CRM to thousands of employees, distribution partners, and even the customers themselves. Also, most organizations at this stage tie together their CRM systems with their ERP (Enterprise Resource Planning) system and other organizational operational systems.

The next stage of CRM will be when systems are designed based on what matters most to the customer and customers will have direct access to all of the information they need in order to do business with an organization. Customer driven CRM means that organizations first understand the customer, and then move inward to operations. The next generation of CRM will also focus more on financial results. Not all customer relationships are profitable and very few companies can afford to deliver an equal level of services to all customers. Organizations must identify existing profitable customer segments and develop the business requirements to support sustained relationships with these profitable segments. However, organizations also need to find cost effective alternatives for current non-buyers or low-margin customers.

Business Intelligence System

Using CRM, a business can:

- Provide better customer service
- Increase customer revenues
- Discover new customers
- Cross sell/Up Sell products more effectively
- Help sales staff close deals faster
- Make call centers more efficient
- Simplify marketing and sales processes

The advantages can be summarized according to the Feature

Marketing

- Make intelligent business decisions with enhanced customer insights
- Increase marketing velocity and speed to market

- Maximize visibility into and control of your entire marketing process
- Drive customer demand
- Increase returns on your marketing investments

Sales

- Grow profitable relationships
- Maintain focus on productive activity
- Eliminate barriers to productivity
- Improve sales efficiency Service
- Transform service into a profitable line of business
- Increase customer loyalty
- Drive revenue
- Reduce costs of customer service and field service
- Decrease service giveaways

Web channel enablement

- Drive revenue and extend market reach
- Increase customer convenience and satisfaction
- Reduce the cost of sales and support
- Build lasting customer loyalty
- Improve sales and service profitability

Running an interaction center

- Increase customer satisfaction
- Improve credibility with your customers
- Increase revenue and productivity
- Manage the customer interaction life cycle

Partner channel management

- Boost revenue through channel collaboration
- Reduce indirect channel support costs
- Increase partner satisfaction and ease of doing business
- Maximize value to your customers by enabling your partners

The types of data CRM projects collect

- Responses to campaigns
- Shipping and fulfillment dates
- Sales and purchase data
- Account information
- Web registration data
- Service and support records
- Demographic data
- Web sales data

Changing patterns of E-CRM solutions in the future

Customer Relationship Management has been corner stone of most organizations as they realize the cost of acquiring new customers is far higher than cost of retaining existing customers. Besides there are other added advantages such as referral sales and customer loyalty. Because reducing customer defection (by little as 5%) will result in increase in profits (by 25% to 85% depending from industry to industry). And the potential loss of a customer over a period of lifetime is huge. Typically in travel loss of a customer over the life time may mean a huge loss. Naturally, organizations are investing heavily to build long term relationship with their customers so that they can continue to enjoy brand loyalty. With new economy emerging and impacting the lifestyles of people across globe, organizations are confronted with a challenge to maintain and nurture the customer relationships to their advantage.

Future CRM solutions will be heavily characterized by:

1. Proactive rather than reactive

2. Personalized care to each individual

3. Heavily technology driven

4. Product and service specific rather than a generic CRM solutions across products and services

5. Shall work on extension of product and service offering beyond the primary product/ service sold

6. CRM solutions shall work on collaborative arrangement among different service offerings so as to cater to the complex needs of individuals

While some of the aspects such as personalized care have touched above, other concepts have been explained below. For this wherever applicable, illustrations described above have been used to explain the future trend of CRM solutions.

E-CRM Components

- Sales functionality: Contact management profiles and history, account management including activities, order entry, proposal generation

- Sales management functionality: pipeline analysis (forecasting, sales cycle analysis, temporary alignment and assignment, roll up and drill down reporting).

- Telemarketing/Telesales functionality: call list assembly, auto dialing, scripting, order taking.

- Time management functionality: single user and group calendar/scheduling, e-mail

- Customer service and support functionality: incident assignment, escalation, tracking/reporting, problem management/resolution, order management/promising, warranty/contract management

- Marketing functionality: campaign management, opportunity management, web-based encyclopedia, configuration, market segmentation, lead generations/enhancement/tracking.

- Executive information functionality: extensive and easy-to-use reporting

- ERP integration functionality: legacy systems, the web, third party external information

- Data synchronization functionality: mobile synchronization with multiple field devices, enterprise synchronization with multiple databases/application servers

- E-commerce functionality: manages procurement through EDI link and web-server and includes B2B and B2C applications

- Service support functionality: Worker orders, dispatching, real time information transfer to field personnel via mobile technologies

The future belongs to those companies who sustain the commitment, investment and organizational agility in becoming customer-centric. They will attract more loyal and profitable customers. They will become havens for more loyal and productive employees and they will be richly rewarded by investors. Strategic use of CRM technology will be a distinguishing feature of these leading companies. And the improving economic climate will be a harbinger for their more rapid emergence.

UNIT:4

CUSTOMER RELATIONSHIP MANAGEMENT PRACTICES

CRM in Financial Services, Measuring Pay back on Customer Relationship Management, Customer Relationship management in FMCG

CRM IN FINANCIAL SERVICES SECTOR

CRM is one of the primary initiatives in any industry and more so in financial industry sector, where competitive pressures from both financial and non-financial services are fueling the movement toward CRM as the companies are systematically raiding a bank's territory to pick-off the most profitable customers. Thus, one has to begin with a financial institution's strategic goals, develop a consistent technology platform that is scalable and support across delivery channels, train people at all levels and incorporate a customer-centric approach to every customer interaction. This article gives an overall picture of CRM with reference to financial service industry.

Customer relationship management (CRM) is one of the primary strategic initiatives in industry today, regardless of whether the company serves retail or wholesale customers, whether it provides services or manufactured goods. In the financial industry, the movement towards CRM (also known as ERM for enterprise relationship management) is being fueled by competitive pressures from both financial and non-financial services companies that are systematically raiding a bank's territory to pick off most valuable customers. Although CRM is not a technology, modern high-tech applications, from relational databases, to data mining, to computer telephony integration (CTI), to Internet delivery channels, are providing the means to implement customer relationship strategies today.

Estimates on the size of the CRM market vary, possibly because of the difficulty in defining CRM. International Data Group predicts the CRM market will grow from $1.9bn in1998 to $11 bn by 2003. AMR Research says the CRM market will grow from $2.3 bn in sales in 1998 to $ 16.8 bn in 2003.

Defining CRM

One of the greatest problems with CRM is what it means. "The whole CRM concept means different people, depending on what they want to do," says Jimmy Sawyers, consultant, Reynolds, Bone & Griesbeck, Memphis, TN.

- **Financial services** that are transaction based, such as credit card companies or bill payment providers, want to manage the customer relationship to drive up transaction volumes and squeeze out expenses from individual transactions. One customer generally has one account and it doesn't matter if others within the same household have accounts. The goal is to provide incentives that get the customer to use the service more. Transactions become commodities. The customer responds to price incentives and loyalty programs. There is almost no opportunity to cross-sell to the individual customer.

- **Consultative financial services,** such as investment advisors and financial planners, use CRM to deepen the trust the customer has in the service provider in order to increase the fees for services. These companies earn fees regardless of the number of transactions the customer makes. They may be able to increase their fees base by cross-selling additional financial services to individuals, or obtaining additional relationships from the same household.

- **Retail oriented financial institution** defines CRM as a combination of the two extremes- managing the entire customer relationship in order to reduce costs and increase the depth of the relationship with the customer. Generally, reducing costs means getting the customer to use less expensive delivery channels. Increasing the customer relationship means either obtaining a larger "share of wallet," or increasing the number of fee-based services the customer uses, or both.

- Any CRM program has three possible financial outcomes:

1. Increased profits

2. Break-even

3. Lost revenue

For some companies, simply knowing that, after deploying CRM, their sales figures exceeded the industry average is enough. For others, the inevitable executive questions loom large – large enough to mandate tangible benefits.

Measuring Pay back on Customer Relationship Management

Can CRM Drive Revenue ?

The important considerations of any organization looking forward to incorporating a CRM are understandably, more business related than technical. Thankfully, all the different objectives that are fulfilled through CRM, by default; revolve around increasing the top line revenue. CRM is not just a guarantee for quicker growth and bigger revenues but also a means to keep up with competition. Through CRM, you can determine the Customer Lifetime Value or in other words, the present and projected business worth of a customer to your organization. This once known, acts as the basis on which you can formulate marketing strategies targeting customers individually.

Customer intelligence and CRMs predictive analysis capabilities help you generate a highly accurate demand forecast which leads to better and more informed inventory management, thus, curtailing significantly, the internal costs through new and efficient processes. Further, the simplification and streamlining of the sales process, significantly reduces the time spent by sales reps on their paperwork and administrative engagements, and lets them focus on selling instead. The ROI gained out of implementing a CRM is what makes the experience worthwhile. It is best measured by comparing the past and the present customer acquisitions, enhancements in customer value/worth, long-term customer retention, etc, all of which contribute to the organizations revenues.

Key Challenges in implementing CRM solutions Companies around the world have leveraged CRM strategies to gain competitive advantage. As more and more companies rush to implement CRM, precautions must be taken to do it right. It is approximated that 50-70% CRM implementations fail, depending on the Industry vertical. Hence, it is essential to identify the key challenges, address risks and build a strategy that can make your CRM successful. CRM is full of talk about strategy, but at the end of the day, someone has to lead the way and implement Even if operations report that the network is operating perfectly and services are running normally, your customers may not be happy, leading to revenue shortfall and increasing levels of churn. You need to view your network and services from your customers' perspective to gain a true understanding of availability, performance, quality and usage. That understanding has to be built from an analysis of each individual's experience. Individual users have different handsets, use different services, connect from different locations, and connect over different paths through the network. They each have individual experiences that you cannot interpret by looking at aggregate metrics and reports. Agilent OSS provides Customer Experience Management, based on the analysis and correlation of individual customer transactions captured by monitoring the signaling traffic buried in your network. Signaling is the central nervous system of your network. It manages every customer activity, from switching on a handset, to downloading ringtones and the most complex inter-operator roaming services. Tapping into this data source gives you the detailed intelligence to optimize your customers' experience of your network and services.

Customer Relationship management in FMCG

There are 3 areas we will explore for management involvement that puts the "icing on the cake", on your customer satisfaction survey program.

1. Customer Satisfaction: A Key Performance Indicator. To effectively manage their business, executives track key performance indicators (KPIs) in the areas of financial performance, sales results, product/service delivery intervals, quality, customer and employee retention, etc. To complete this picture, you need to bring executive attention to your company's customer satisfaction levels. If these are not on the list of metrics, that your senior management team monitors, you are encouraged to increase awareness of the benefits of doing so. If you require more information, regarding the relationship between increasing customer satisfaction and increases in

revenue, to "promote the cause", give us a call. We would be happy to share additional information on this topic.

2. Ensure customer-focused change programs are in line with strategy. Your business, like most, is changing every day. This requires senior management to continuously evaluate where and how resources are invested. The customer survey remediation program (described in a previous article) will generate many ideas for initiatives to improve customer satisfaction levels.

Management must be aware of, and at some level "approve", these programs to ensure that they are in line with corporate direction. In an environment of stretched resources, as is especially the case today, when you make a decision to say "yes" to a new initiative, you are required to make a decision of "no", to what you will no longer focus on. Make no mistake, this decision WILL occur: either consciously or unconsciously. These decisions are much better made on a conscious level based on the priorities you have set for your organization.

3. Customer Feedback: Critical Input to Business Decisions. Often companies review market trends to look

for opportunities to augment their product and service offerings with the hope of capturing "new revenue" from "new customers". And, they do this without an understanding of what they could achieve for "new revenue" from their existing customer-base.

Existing methods for taking the customer's perspective several tools already exist that can help one take the customer's view. They originate in the disciplines of marketing, consumer behavior, new consumer thinking and user-centered design. Marketing as a discipline considers cultural, social, personal and psychological factors when analyzing consumer markets. Marketing also helps take the customer's view using market segments that group customers by geography, demographic characteristics - like age, life-cycle stage, gender, income, generation, and social class, psychographic characteristics (such as lifestyle, personality & values) and behavioral patterns like - occasions, product usage rate, and loyalty amongst others.

Consumer behavior is an obviously important component of the overall subject, typically emphasizing the purchasing activity within a combined process and influence model. It generally covers the consumer buying process and attempts to understand how it is influenced by the consumer's personal, psychological and social factors.

An organization cannot design effective customer experiences that reinforce the brand without a process-based infrastructure that enables the delivery platforms to execute the strategy. Product, people and process must be built around the value and needs of the customer base in order to ensure that the customer experience is measurable and trackable for the company, while relevant and consistent for the customer. At the same time, these are the means from which the brand reaches the end-customer, ensuring that both the externally facing customer interactions—as well as the internal processes that enable the experiences—are designed from the customer's perspective. Nikon is an example of a company at the forefront of understanding the impact of consistency on brand.